THINK BIG!

THE GREATEST IDEAS IN
TECHNOLOGY

SONYA NEWLAND

WAYLAND
www.waylandbooks.co.uk

First published in Great Britain in 2022 by Wayland
Copyright © Hodder and Stoughton, 2022

Produced for Wayland by
White-Thomson Publishing Ltd
www.wtpub.co.uk

HB ISBN 978 1 5263 1693 6
PB ISBN 978 15263 1694 3

Editor: Sonya Newland
Designer: Rocket Design (East Anglia) Ltd

The publisher would like to thank the following for permission to reproduce their pictures:
Alamy: 12r (Chris Willson), 15b (David Gee 4), 18r (The History Collection), 27t (dpa picture alliance); Getty: 4b (Bettman), 7t (Bettmann), 9t (The Asahi Shimbun), 12l (Keystone), 14l (Justin Sullivan), 22b (All About Space Magazine), 23b (Pier Marco Tacca); NASA: 10l, 10r, 11l, 24l (MSFC), 24r (JSC), 25b (KSC/Tony Gray and Tim Powers); Shutterstock: 4t (James Steidl), 5 (elenabsl), 7bl (Everett Collection), 7br (Vasyl Shulga), 8t (icosha), 8b (tackune), 9b (cyo bo), 13 (hanohiki), 14r (Artist Vaska), 15tl (Forrester Images Ltd), 15tr (Tarzhanova), 16t (AFANASEV IVAN), 16b (drserg), 17tl (Nuch Rp), 17tr (oxygendesign021), 17b (fizkes), 18l (Uuganaa), 19b (J. Lekavicius), 20t (lola1960), 20m (rehab-icons), 20b (evgdemidova), 21t (WAYHOME studio), 21b (marleyPug), 22t (D-VISIONS), 23t (D-VISIONS), 25t (Nerthuz), 26l (oasisamuel), 26r (Constantine Pankin), 27b (Elnur), 28t (fizkes), 28b (Marina Dekhnik), 29t (olesia_g), 29t (metamorworks); Julian Baker: 6, 19t; White-Thomson Publishing: 11r.

All design elements from Shutterstock.

Printed in China

Wayland
An imprint of
Hachette Children's Group
Part of Hodder and Stoughton
Carmelite House
50 Victoria Embankment
London EC4Y 0DZ

An Hachette UK Company
www.hachette.co.uk
www.hachettechildrens.co.uk

Contents

Technology

It is impossible to imagine our world without technology. It's all around us — in how we learn, work, relax, communicate, travel and much more. Every minute of every day, scientists and engineers all over the world are coming up with technological ideas to make our lives better, easier and more efficient.

Where do we begin?

What we think of as technology today is probably quite different to ideas about it in the past. Now, in the third decade of the 21st century, 'technology' usually refers to computers, robots, smart devices — amazing machines controlled by electronics. But look back 100 years, or 500 years, or thousands of years and technology was very different. At some point in the past, even the basic wheel was cutting-edge technology!

GENIUS

The history of technology has been dominated by the ideas of men rather than women. That's changing now, but some inspirational women made their mark in the past, too. English mathematician Ada Lovelace (1815–52) is famous for her work on the earliest computers in the 1840s. In the 1940s, American computer scientist Grace Hopper (1906–92) was one of the first to develop computer programming languages.

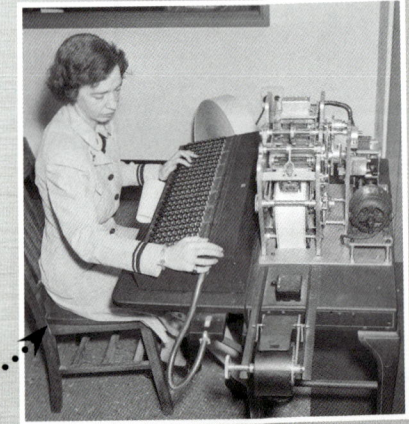

Grace Hopper ••••••••••

Thinking big

Not every idea is a huge success. Some don't work well enough. Some just aren't what people want. Some are popular for a while but then are overtaken by a better idea. It takes time to know if an idea really is a big one! Success lies in how well the technology fulfils its purpose and, often, how easily it can be adapted to incorporate new ideas and needs. This book explores some of the more recent ideas in technology that have had a lasting impact on the world.

THINK BIG!

Do some research to find out about technology that seemed like a big idea at the start, but didn't stand the test of time. You could begin by looking up one or more of the following:

- **MiniDiscs**
- **Betamax**
- **Microsoft Zune**
- **Nintendo Virtual Boy**
- **Hoverboards**

Why do you think these ideas seemed ground-breaking when they were created? Can you think of any improvements that might have made them more successful? What big ideas do you have for new technology that might improve people's lives?

Televisor

When Scottish inventor John Logie Baird demonstrated the machine he called the 'televisor' in 1926, it was the first time the public had seen moving images on the small screen. Baird's device changed the face of entertainment technology forever.

The big idea

Like a lot of great inventions, the televisor developed the work of earlier inventors. In 1884, the German engineer Paul Nipkow had worked out a way of scanning images using moving discs. In 1907, fellow German Arthur Korn designed the first electrical circuits that could transmit images. Baird adapted these ideas to create the first television.

How did it work?

The trick to Baird's mechanical television was converting light into electrical impulses and back again.

2. Light was focused through the disc onto the subject (here, the woman).

3. The light reflected off the subject onto a photoelectric cell, which turned it into electrical impulses.

4. The electrical impulses were sent to a transmitter.

5. They passed to a receiver and then to a neon tube, positioned behind another disc.

1. A motor turned a disc that had a spiral of holes punched in it.

6. The impulses appeared as areas of dark and light on a screen, forming an image.

GENIUS

John Logie Baird (1888–1946) was interested in electronics from an early age. As a boy, he even built a telephone exchange so he could speak to his friends! Baird began working on ways to send moving images and sound in 1920, using basic materials such as cardboard, string and a bicycle lamp. It was these early experiments that led to his television breakthrough.

John Logie Baird with his televisor

Where did it lead?

Baird later invented colour TV and made the first long-distance television transmission. But image quality on these early mechanical televisions was poor, and soon electronic TVs took over. But even today's wide-screen, high-definition televisions owe their existence to Baird's big idea.

Early TVs were tiny, especially compared to today's wide-screen models. Some were only 7 cm wide!

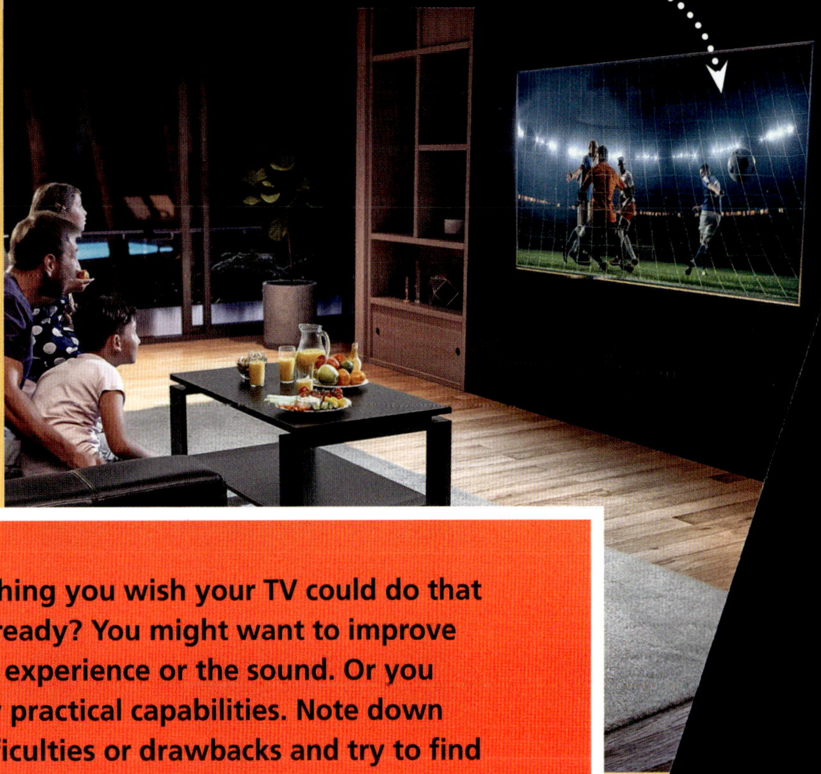

THINK BIG!

Is there anything you wish your TV could do that it doesn't already? You might want to improve the viewing experience or the sound. Or you might want to give it new practical capabilities. Note down your ideas, then identify any difficulties or drawbacks and try to find some solutions. Include some sketches of your design.

Shinkansen 'bullet train'

Engineers and inventors are constantly working on ways to create more efficient forms of transport. One of the most successful ideas of the 20th century was the amazing bullet train, which led to the world's first high-speed rail network.

The big idea

In the 1800s, the first railways revolutionised transport, allowing people to reach distant destinations much more quickly than the traditional horse and carriage. By the mid-1900s, however, people wanted to travel further and faster. So, engineers in Japan began to consider how to build really high-speed trains.

Bullet trains are so-called because the front of the train has the streamlined shape of a bullet.

How did it work?

As it turned out, the engineers had to design more than just the trains. Existing tracks could not be adapted to fit the new carriages, so a whole new network had to be designed.

...re 'air-sealed', so that the air ...e them stays the same when ...tunnels at high speed.

Shinkansen trains are bigger than normal trains.

There is a special 'power car', or engine, at each end.

High-speed rail tracks are made of stronger materials than traditional tracks.

GENIUS

Mechanical engineer Hideo Shima (1901–98) began by designing steam engines for the Japanese Ministry of Railways. He was promoted to chief engineer there, and played a key role in the design of the Shinkansen network. Later, Shima became head of Japan's National Space Agency.

Where did it lead?

The Shinkansen made its first journey in 1964. With a top speed of 210 km/h, it cut the journey time between the cities of Tokyo and Osaka in half, to 3 hours and 10 minutes. Travel times have improved even more since then. Today, bullet trains can just about beat 300 km/h. But there are plans for a high-speed maglev train – one that uses 'magnetic levitation' technology to run. The maglev's top speed of around 600 km/h will leave all other trains standing!

THINK BIG!

Do some research to find out how maglev trains work and why they can travel even faster than trains on traditional tracks. Design an experiment to show the difference. You could use magnets to create a maglev train and track, and design an ordinary track using a material such as wood. Can you think of any ways to improve each system?

Strong magnets cause maglev trains to 'float' above the tracks. This reduces friction, and makes for a faster, smoother ride.

Without Saturn V, one of the biggest technological achievements of the 20th century might never have happened. This rocket launched NASA's Apollo space missions in the 1960s and 1970s – including Apollo 11, which put the first men on the Moon.

The big idea

In 1961, US President John F. Kennedy announced that the USA would send men to the Moon by the end of the decade. That was a big dream considering how little was known about space travel at the time. The US space agency NASA turned to German rocket engineer Wernher von Braun for some bright ideas on how to make this happen.

GENIUS

Von Braun was the brains behind Saturn V's design, but Katherine Johnson (1918–2020) was the unsung hero of NASA's Moon missions. She was the genius mathematician who worked out the flight paths of the Apollo spacecraft. Success or failure – and the lives of the astronauts – rested on Johnson's work.

Saturn V was 111 m tall and weighed 2.8 million kg.

How did it work?

Reaching the Moon would require a massive rocket. And even if a big enough rocket could be built, how could it carry enough fuel to reach the speeds of 400,000 km/h it needed to escape Earth's gravity? Von Braun had the answers. He designed the Saturn V in three stages. Each stage split off when it ran out of fuel.

The Stage 3 engines carried enough fuel to get the Apollo craft into Earth's orbit and send it off towards the Moon.

Stage 2's engines would then fire up, giving the rocket enough boost to almost reach Earth's orbit.

Stage 1 lifted the rocket to an altitude of about 68 km, then broke away.

Where did it lead?

What scientists and engineers learnt from Saturn V and the Apollo missions influenced all later space technology and travel. It opened up exploration of our solar system and beyond. Today, private companies as well as governments are working on space travel – and even space tourism.

Saturn V's final launch carried the first US space station, Skylab, into orbit in 1973.

THINK BIG!

One of the key principles of rocket science is Isaac Newton's third law of motion: for every action there is an equal and opposite reaction. When a rocket releases fuel from its engine, the rocket lifts off in the opposite direction. Design and carry out an experiment to test this law and see how rockets move. You could use a balloon, with air as your fuel.

Motorola DynaTAC

There are more than 5.2 billion mobile phone users in the world today — that's around two-thirds of the global population. So it's hard to believe that just 40 years ago that number was zero! It was only in the early 1980s that Motorola turned the idea of a phone you could carry around into a reality.

The big idea

Wireless phone technology had existed since the 1940s, but the phones themselves weren't exactly portable. They needed such huge amounts of power that only a car battery could keep them charged, so the earliest 'mobile' phones were installed in vehicles. In 1968, hearing that its rival, AT&T, was working on a truly portable phone, electronics company Motorola established a team to do the same.

How did it work?

The DynaTAC (Dynamic Adaptive Total Area Coverage) phone was announced in 1973. But it was another ten years before it was made available to the public, in the 8000X model.

Some cars in the 1950s and 1960s were fitted with phones, but they were big — and expensive!

Cost: £3,000

Length: 33 cm

Display: LCD

Phonebook memory: 30

Battery life: 30 minutes talk time

Weight: 784 g

Time to charge: 10 hours

GENIUS

American engineer Martin Cooper (b. 1928) led the DynaTAC team. He had made his mark at Motorola in the 1960s with projects such as the first radio-controlled traffic-light system. Just before the DynaTAC was publicly announced, Cooper used it to make the first ever mobile phone call – to the head of AT&T's rival project! Cooper later established his own wireless technology companies.

Where did it lead?

Later developments saw the DynaTAC evolve to have an LED display and longer battery life. However, the DynaTAC was an analogue phone, so after digital took over in the 1990s, Motorola's pioneering device was discontinued. Digital technology developed rapidly, and led to the amazing devices we have today – phones that are not just mobile, but smart too.

Today, mobile phones go with us everywhere, allowing instant communication and access to information wherever we are.

THINK BIG!

When planning their next-generation phones, designers and engineers think about two main things:

• How can existing features be improved?
• What new, useful features can be added?

Look at your phone with these two questions in mind. Write down any ideas you have. Think carefully – are your ideas just gimmicks, or will users genuinely find them useful? Draw some diagrams or sketches to show your phone upgrades.

Apple Macintosh

The Apple Mac may not have been the first ever personal computer, but it was the one that changed the face of personal computing. Released in 1984, the Macintosh 128K was the first computer to have a built-in screen, a mouse and a graphical user interface (GUI).

The big idea

Steve Jobs and Steve Wozniak started computer company Apple in 1976 and launched the Apple I later that year. This was followed by the Apple II in 1977. Both models were successful, but Jobs wanted something different – a computer that people would find both easy and instinctive to use. And so the Macintosh was born.

When the Apple I launched, Wozniak built every computer by hand!

GENIUS

Graphic designer Susan Kare (b. 1954) was the bright mind behind the original icons in Apple's ground-breaking GUI. Her simple, friendly designs made it easy to navigate and understand the computer. They included the bomb when the system crashed, the 'happy Mac' icon and the 'feature' symbol – still used as the command key today.

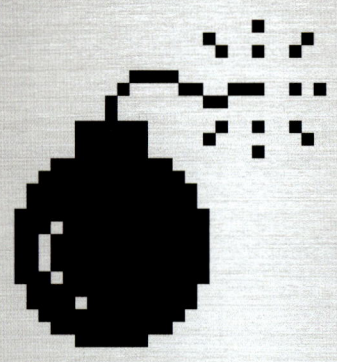

The Macintosh 128K

The 9-inch black-and-white screen had 512 x 342 pixels.

It had 128K of Random Access Memory (RAM) — increased to 512K in the second model.

There was no hard drive. The original Mac had to be started up from a floppy disk!

It came with a one-button mouse.

How did it work?

Existing computers used a text-based command-line interface, which meant that users had to type in commands. Macintosh's GUI allowed users to click on icons to access files and operate software.

Where did it lead?

The Macintosh was undoubtedly attractive, but it was expensive, slow and incompatible with a lot of software. Jobs and Wozniak quickly moved on to the next generation. Today, there are many types of Apple Mac available, but they are all descendants of the original 128K.

The first iMac was launched in 1998. iMacs are still on sale — although they look a lot different!

THINK BIG!

What do you think personal computers will be like in the future? Perhaps all computers will be custom-designed for their users. Design a computer that matches your own needs. Think about what you need it to do — and what you don't! What will it look like? How big should it be?

🌐 World Wide Web

The World Wide Web is a huge system of information, stored on and retrieved from the global network of computers we call the internet. When software engineer Tim Berners-Lee launched this big idea, no one could have guessed how it would go on to transform the world.

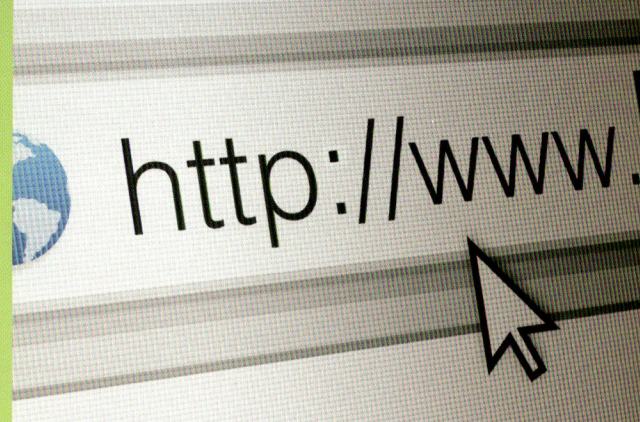

The first website addresses all included the letters www, but it's not necessary to include them today.

The big idea

In 1989, Berners-Lee was working at the famous European Organization for Nuclear Research (CERN) in Switzerland. He wanted scientists there – and all over the world – to be able to share information easily. The internet already existed, but there was no way of linking the documents on it. Berners-Lee realised that he could use a technology called HyperText to make that happen.

GENIUS

Tim Berners-Lee (b. 1955) began his career creating software for printers. By 1980, he was working at CERN, where he helped to develop a program for sharing information – an idea he later built on to create the World Wide Web. Berners-Lee is now the director of the World Wide Web Consortium. This international group manages the web, ensuring it can be shared by everyone.

How did it work?

Berners-Lee used three key technologies to make sure that all the computers on the internet could understand each other: HTML, URL (or URI) and HTTP.

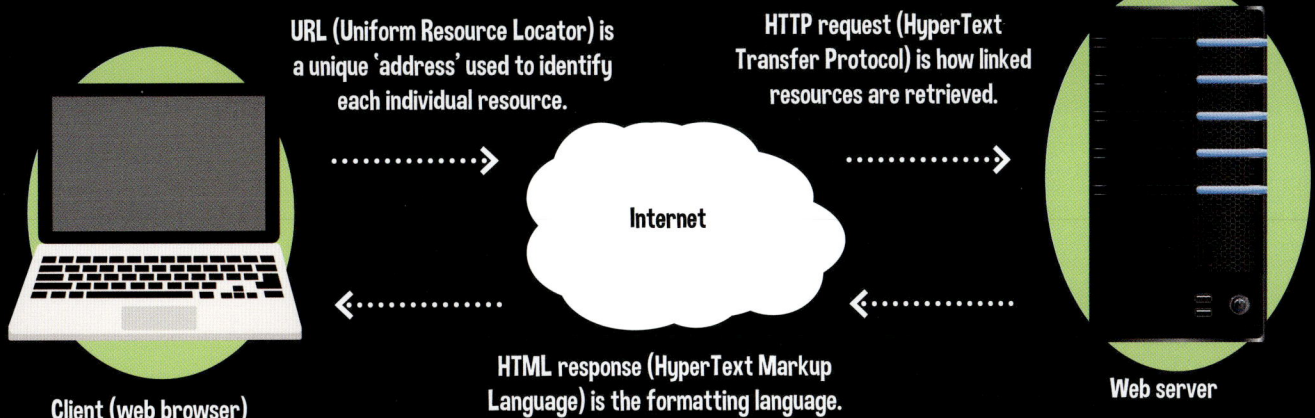

URL (Uniform Resource Locator) is a unique 'address' used to identify each individual resource.

HTTP request (HyperText Transfer Protocol) is how linked resources are retrieved.

Internet

HTML response (HyperText Markup Language) is the formatting language.

Client (web browser)

Web server

Where did it lead?

Does a day go by when you don't look something up using the internet? The World Wide Web had an extraordinary impact, permanently changing the way people access and share information. And those three key technologies that Berners-Lee used more than 30 years ago are still the basis for the web today!

There are already more than 1.8 billion websites on the World Wide Web – and around 150 new websites are being added every minute!

There are lots of online programs that help you build your own website. Try Wix or Site123, or search for a program you like (get an adult to help you). Decide what you want your website to be about – it could be a blog about music, books or films, or an information website about a sport or hobby you enjoy. Remember to choose the text, images and layouts carefully as you design your website.

17

Toyota Prius

For most of the 20th century, almost all road vehicles were powered by petrol. The arrival of the first hybrid car, the Prius, in 1997, set the vehicle manufacturing industry on a new track – towards a whole range of more environmentally friendly cars.

The big idea

The gases released by petrol-powered cars cause air pollution and contribute to global warming. This is bad for people's health and for the environment. So, engineers began looking for ways to reduce the use of petrol. One of the best ideas was to create a hybrid – a car powered by both petrol and electricity. The Japanese company Toyota was the first to get a hybrid car to market.

GENIUS

The idea of a vehicle that used both electricity and petrol was actually more than 100 years old by the time the Prius came along. German car engineer Ferdinand Porsche (1875–1951) designed the first hybrid vehicle in 1898. Unfortunately the 'Lohner-Porsche Mixed Hybrid' wasn't very popular, so hybrid cars didn't take off at the time.

The Lohner-Porsche had electric motors in the wheel hubs.

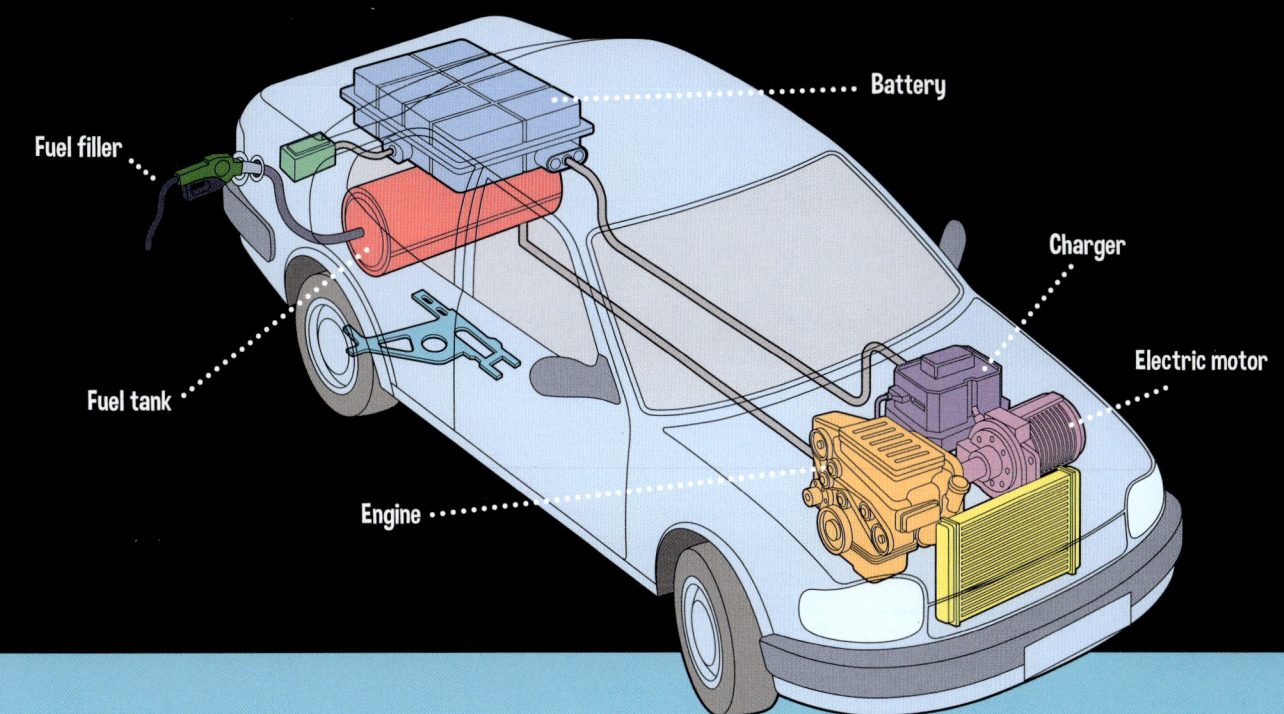

Battery

Charger

Electric motor

Fuel filler

Fuel tank

Engine

How did it work?

The first model Prius wasn't a great success. Acceleration was poor, emissions were still quite high and, like Porsche's original hybrid, people just didn't seem too keen on it! But Toyota worked hard to improve the design and performance to make it a car that everyone wanted.

Where did it lead?

Toyota knew their car would lead the way for other hybrids – the name Prius even means 'to go before' in Latin. Today, many manufacturers make hybrid cars and even fully electric cars. In the not-too-distant future, petrol-powered cars will probably be found only in museums!

How do you think cars and other vehicles could be improved? You might come up with ways for them to be more environmentally friendly – or just more user-friendly! Note down some ideas, then pick one and design your own car of the future. Think about the different materials it should be made from, and how it would be used.

Electric charging points for hybrid and electric cars are now a common sight in many countries.

🎧 MP3

Music formats have been through several stages of evolution since vinyl records became popular in the first half of the 20th century. Cassette tapes and compact discs (CDs) both enjoyed huge success. But it was the creation of the digital format MP3 that forever changed how we hear and share music.

The big idea

In the late 1980s, digital technology was developing rapidly. Experts wondered if they could transmit music files through digital telephone lines. To do so, the files needed to be much smaller. The German company Fraunhofer-Gesellschaft began figuring out how to reduce the size of audio files without losing sound quality. The team that made the breakthrough, in 1988, was called the Moving Picture Experts Group, which is where the MPEG gets its name.

GENIUS

Karlheinz Brandenburg (b. 1954) is known as the 'father of MP3'. He led the team at Fraunhofer-Gesellschaft that eventually came up with the compression technology in the late 1980s. His research formed the basis of other audio technology too, including AAC (Advanced Audio Coding).

A compression algorithm reduces the file size so it can be stored on a digital device.

It achieves this by removing the parts of the audio that the human ear can't detect.

It is called a 'lossy' format because data is removed and the compression can't be reversed.

A three-minute song in a lossless file is around 30 megabytes (MB). Compressed to an MP3 file, that song is only 3 MB.

How did it work?

In simple terms, an audio file is converted to code that splits it into layers. The layers can then be saved or removed depending on whether the sound in that layer is really important. The process is called MPEG Audio Layer 3, so the resulting file is known as an MP3.

Where did it lead?

By the mid-1990s, MP3 had really taken off. Files could be transferred quickly and easily, so there was a huge increase in file sharing. It was a great way for people to access music, but it was also easier to share files illegally. Today, digital recordings are closely controlled to prevent this. Digital downloads are now the main way that people buy music, and streaming services such as Spotify are hugely popular.

Soon, devices were created specifically to play digital music, including the Apple iPod, which was launched in 2001.

THINK BIG!

Each development over the past 100 years – vinyl records, cassette tapes, CDs and even MiniDiscs – has improved on the previous one in some way. So, where is there left to go with music formats? Do some research into the quality and versatility of MP3 compared to these older formats. How could digital music files be improved?

Large Hadron Collider

The idea behind the world's most powerful particle accelerator, the Large Hadron Collider (LHC), may be one of the biggest in the world — and even beyond! This amazing machine was designed to help scientists work out the mysteries of our universe.

The big idea

The universe was created by the Big Bang, about 14 billion years ago. In an instant, it expanded from the size of an atom to the size of a galaxy. To fully understand the universe's origins, scientists wanted to recreate its conditions in those very first seconds. To do that, they needed to make beams of tiny particles called hadrons collide.

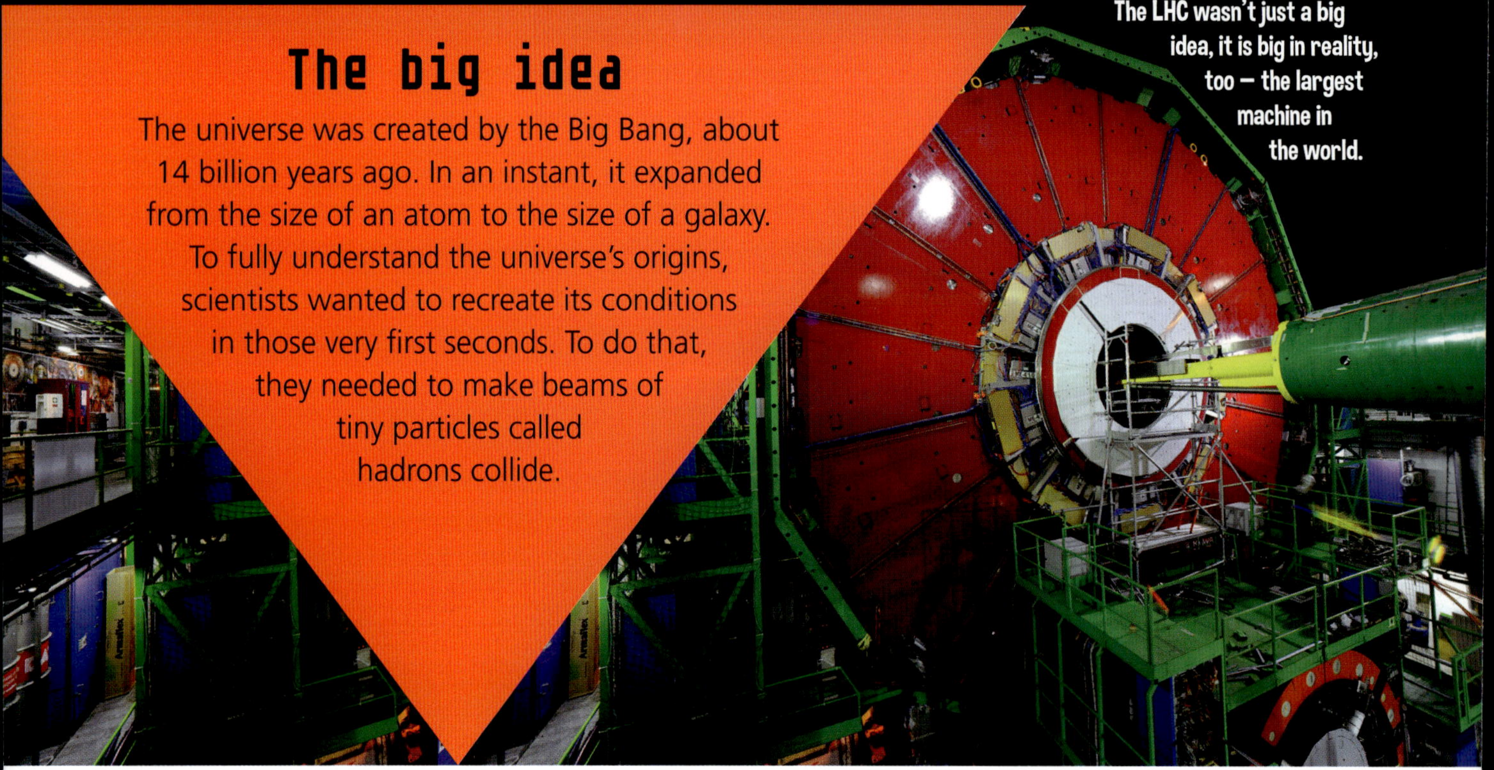

The LHC wasn't just a big idea, it is big in reality, too — the largest machine in the world.

How did it work?

The LHC was built at CERN in Switzerland (see page 16). It lies 100 m below ground, and consists of a 27-km ring of 'superconducting' magnets.

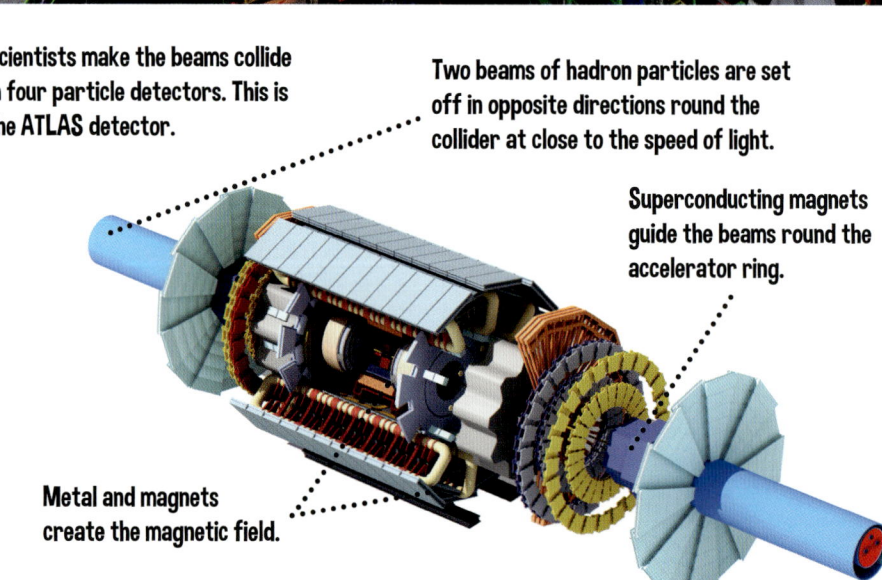

Scientists make the beams collide in four particle detectors. This is the ATLAS detector.

Two beams of hadron particles are set off in opposite directions round the collider at close to the speed of light.

Superconducting magnets guide the beams round the accelerator ring.

Metal and magnets create the magnetic field.

Where did it lead?

The LHC has already helped with some ground-breaking discoveries, including a previously unknown particle, the Higgs boson. But this is just the start. So far, the LHC has collected only a tiny percentage of all the data it is capable of gathering. Other countries and groups are now developing circular colliders like the LHC. What other amazing mysteries might they reveal?

GENIUS

Fabiola Gianotti (b. 1960) became a research scientist at CERN in 1994. Since then she has helped to develop and build particle accelerators, conduct experiments and analyse the important information they have revealed. In 2012, she explained how the LHC had proved existence of the Higgs boson, a particle which – in simple terms – gives everything in the universe its mass. In 2016, Gianotti became the first female Director-General of CERN.

THINK BIG!

Not all particle detectors are as huge and complicated as the LHC. In fact, you can build your own particle detector in the form of a cloud chamber. Search online for instructions on creating a cloud chamber (there is one suggestion on page 31). Conduct your experiment and analyse your results. What have you learnt about the world around you at an atomic level? What else would you like to know?

International Space Station

Russia was the first country to launch a space station in the 1960s, but the space laboratory known as the International Space Station (ISS) was the first international effort. It is the only space station in operation today.

The big idea

Early space stations showed the value of having a laboratory in Earth's orbit. But scientists wanted something more permanent – a place for astronauts to base themselves for longer periods of time to do extended research. To achieve this goal, five space agencies representing 15 different countries all worked together to build the ISS.

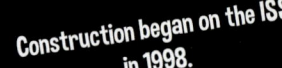
Construction began on the ISS in 1998.

GENIUS

Peggy Whitson (b. 1960) was an American astronaut. Her first mission to the ISS was in 2002, and she spent 185 days there. She made history by becoming the first woman in charge of the ISS on her second posting in 2007, during which she performed five ETAs (space walks) to improve the station's living and working areas.

Peggy Whitson was the most experienced astronaut at NASA when she retired in 2018.

The ISS orbits 4,000 km above Earth, completing one orbit every 90 minutes.

How did it work?

It took 10 years and more than 30 space missions to fully build the ISS, but it was an amazing technological achievement.

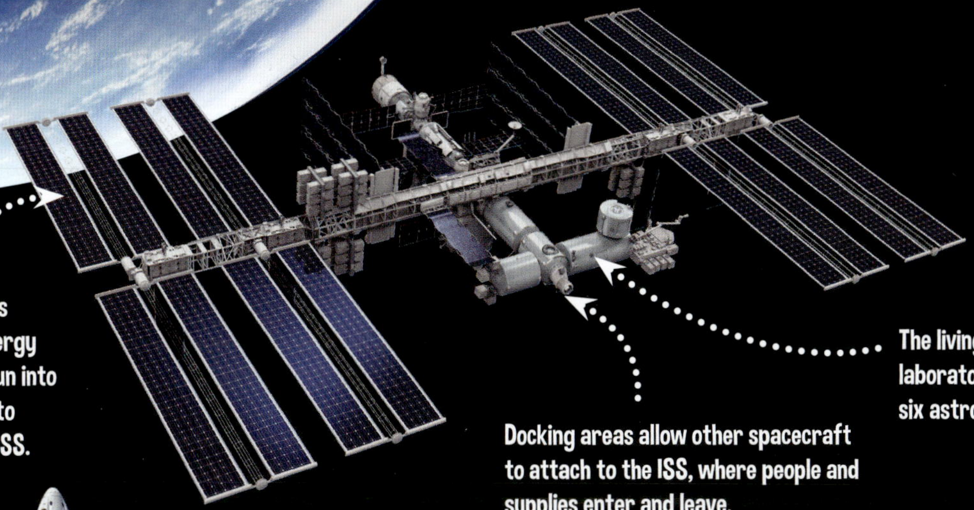

Solar panels convert energy from the Sun into electricity to power the ISS.

Docking areas allow other spacecraft to attach to the ISS, where people and supplies enter and leave.

The living areas and laboratories can house six astronauts at a time.

Where did it lead?

Astronauts have been living on the ISS constantly since 2000 – even before construction was completed. The experiments carried out there have already taught us a lot about space technology and how the human body copes in the space environment. What else might these space scientists learn in the future?

In 2020, SpaceX's Dragon spacecraft launched for the ISS, where it became the first privately owned space vehicle to visit the space station.

Think of something that would be useful for scientists to know about how the human body functions in space. Design an experiment that could be carried out on the ISS to test it. Research what conditions are like both in space and on the ISS to give you some ideas.

Nest Learning Thermostat

Wireless technology improved rapidly in the early 21st century, and engineers began to think of new ways to use it. With environmental issues taking centre stage, it was natural that they would look at developing devices to save energy. Nest Labs came up with a smart, self-learning thermostat which did just that.

The big idea

When coming up with new uses for wireless tech, engineers began with the basics. What things in our daily lives would it be useful to control from a distance? Household gadgets that benefited both people and the environment – by saving energy, for example – topped that list. Nest Labs thought it would be great if you could turn on the heating when you left work so the house was nice and warm when you arrived home.

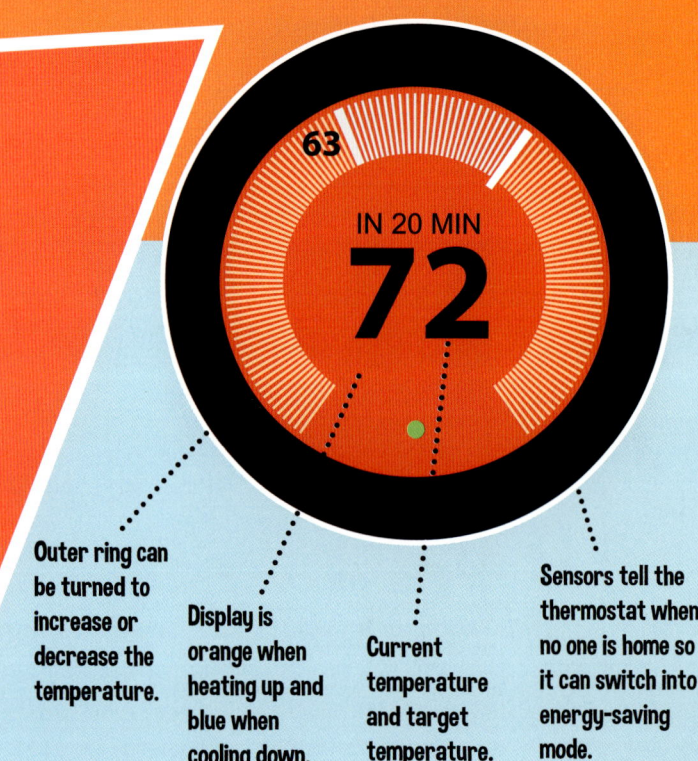

Outer ring can be turned to increase or decrease the temperature.

Display is orange when heating up and blue when cooling down.

Current temperature and target temperature.

Sensors tell the thermostat when no one is home so it can switch into energy-saving mode.

The thermostat can be controlled remotely using a mobile phone app.

How did it work?

The Nest Learning Thermostat uses intelligent technology to work out a heating routine that perfectly suits individual users. For the first week, you programme the thermostat manually. An algorithm learns your routines, preferred temperatures and times. Then it works on its own!

GENIUS

American engineer Tony Fadell (b. 1969) was building his own energy-efficient home, but became frustrated by how thermostats didn't offer energy-saving features. He started Nest Labs in 2010, where he pioneered the development of the Learning Thermostat. After Google bought Nest, Fadell moved on to Future Shape, a business that helps small companies working on green and other new technologies.

Where did it lead?

When it was launched in 2011, the Nest Thermostat used ground-breaking smart technology. Now that kind of tech is common throughout our homes. Lights, sound systems and other electronics can all now be controlled wirelessly and connected in one big smart home. But new ideas and technology are being developed all the time, and existing ones are being improved, so who knows what might be the next big idea!

What gadgets would you like to be 'smartened up'? Design your own smart device that would make life easier. When you have thought of an idea, find out if any companies are already developing it. What are their plans? Have you thought of similar features and functions?

🎤 Siri

Artificial intelligence (AI) is technology that can learn on its own, without being programmed by humans. You probably interact with AI every day. One of the most common interactions is with a smart virtual personal assistant (VPA), such as Apple's Siri — one of the most popular VPAs in the world.

The big idea

Apple had been thinking about a digital personal assistant since 1987: an interactive helper that could respond to the human voice, answer questions and even learn and adapt. But it wasn't until 2010 that their idea became reality with Siri. Apple has continued to develop the technology, and Siri now responds to both voice and gesture, and uses incredible AI to learn on its own.

Siri was the first widely used virtual assistant. It uses speech recognition software and natural language processing to understand voice commands and respond to requests.

GENIUS

Siri was the brainchild of engineers Adam Cheyer, Dag Kittlaus and Tom Gruber, who worked at the Stanford Research Institute in the USA. When Apple launched the iPhone in 2007, the developers realised they could sell Siri as an app for the phone. Within just a few months, Steve Jobs had recognised what a brilliant idea it was, and he bought the technology for Apple.

How does it work?

VPA developers try to give their products a friendly, helpful personality. A user gets Siri's attention with the wake word 'Hey Siri'. Siri responds: 'What can I help you with?'

1. Siri 'hears' the question or command as sound waves.

2. These are converted to code, which is broken down into key words and phrases.

3. An algorithm translates these to work out what task Siri is being asked to do.

4. Siri can access in-built apps, such as Contacts and Maps, and will search these for answers, or it can search wider via the internet.

5. Text-to-speech technology is used to speak the answer.

Where did it lead?

There are many different voice-activated personal assistants available now – and they're getting smarter by the day! Every time you talk to Siri, you're helping to improve the AI that runs it. Siri can still be used to tell you the weather and remind you about appointments. But it can also control smart gadgets around the home (see pages 26–27). New things are being added to its list of skills all the time.

VPAs can now be used with smart speakers to control all sorts of devices in a smart home.

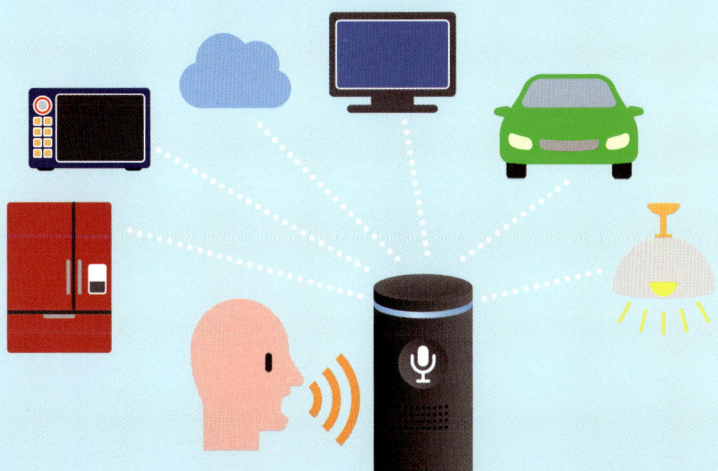

THINK BIG!

Find out more about how Siri and other VPAs 'learn' about you to improve their responses. Devise an experiment that will test how well the device learns. For example, think of some questions or instructions that would help the assistant to know more about you. How effective is it? You might have to carry out this experiment over several weeks for Siri to learn and apply that knowledge.

Glossary

air pollution gases or particles released into the air that have harmful effects

algorithm a set of steps that tell a computer what to do in order to solve a problem or perform a task

analogue describing audio or video signals that are coded as continuous electronic pulses (*see digital*)

Big Bang the moment when the universe was created

digital describing signals that are translated into binary code (*see analogue*)

electronics a branch of physics and technology that designs electrical circuits

electronic television a television where the images are scanned by an electronic camera and received by a cathode-ray tube

friction a natural force that acts on objects moving over each other

global warming the increase in global temperatures over a long period of time

LCD liquid crystal display – a type of device screen that has two layers of special glass though which liquid crystals carry or block light

LED light emitting diodes – the type of lights used in some display screens

manually by hand rather than by machine

mass the amount of matter something contains, measured in grams or kilograms

mechanical television a television in which images are scanned by discs powered by motors

particle accelerator a machine used to speed up the movement of the tiny particles found in atoms

photoelectric cell an electrical device whose features, such as current and resistance, are affected by light

portable describes things that can be carried around easily

software engineer someone who designs and develops computer software

streamlined having a long, thin shape and often a pointed front, to reduce resistance when travelling through air or water

telephone exchange the equipment that connects telephone lines when they are being used by callers

versatility an ability to be adapted to be used in different ways

wake word a particular word or phrase that tells a smart speaker or virtual personal assistant that you want to use it

Further information

Books

AI (The Tech Head Guide) by William Potter (Wayland, 2021)

Digital Technology (Technology Timelines) by Tom Jackson (Franklin Watts, 2016)

Technology (Building the World) by Paul Mason (Wayland, 2020)

Triumphs of Technology (STEM-gineers) by Rob Colson (Wayland, 2018)

Websites

www.nasa.gov/audience/ forstudents/k-4/more_to_explore/ International-Space-Station.html

Find out more about the International Space Station on NASA's website.

www.nasa.gov/audience/ forstudents/5-8/features/nasa-knows/ what-was-the-saturn-v-58.html

Explore the story of the Moon landing, and Saturn V's part in it.

www.symmetrymagazine.org/article/ january-2015/how-to-build-your-own- particle-detector

This website has instructions for creating a particle-detecting cloud chamber.

Index

Titles in the Think Big! series

THE GREATEST IDEAS IN CONSERVATION

- National parks
- Clean Air Act
- DDT ban
- Earth Day
- Project Tiger
- Ozone hole
- Svalbard Seed Vault
- The Ocean Cleanup
- Desert Sunlight Solar Farm
- The Paris Agreement
- School strike for climate
- Biodegradable plastic

THE GREATEST IDEAS IN ENTERTAINMENT

- Technicolor
- Scrabble
- Lego
- Disneyland
- Sony Walkman
- NES
- Live Aid
- Harry Potter
- File streaming
- Streaming services
- *Candy Crush Saga*
- Oculus Rift

THE GREATEST IDEAS IN MEDICINE

- The smallpox vaccine
- Antibiotics
- Transplant surgery
- Pacemakers
- In vitro fertilisation (IVF)
- MRI scanning
- The Global Polio Eradication Initiative
- The Human Genome Project
- Stem cell research
- Bionic prosthetics
- Remote surgery
- Immunotherapy

THE GREATEST IDEAS IN TECHNOLOGY

- Televisor
- Shinkansen 'bullet train'
- Saturn V
- Motorola DynaTAC
- Apple Macintosh
- World Wide Web
- Toyota Prius
- MP3
- Large Hadron Collider
- International Space Station
- Nest Learning Thermostat
- Siri